Ibeath's Modern Language Series

FIRST SPANISH COURSE

With Topical Charts, Direct-Method Exercises
and
Alternative English-Spanish Exercises

BY

E. C. HILLS   AND   J. D. M. FORD
UNIVERSITY OF CALIFORNIA   HARVARD UNIVERSITY

NEW EDITION

D. C. HEATH AND COMPANY
BOSTON   NEW YORK   CHICAGO   LONDON
ATLANTA   DALLAS   SAN FRANCISCO

PREFACE TO THE NEW EDITION

In the new edition of the *First Spanish Course* a few modifications have been made in the Lessons and a complete set of Alternative English-Spanish Exercises has been added at the end. Both the new set of exercises and the older set illustrate the grammatical material of the respective Lessons and repeat with variants the subject matter of the Spanish reading texts. The new edition contains an extensive list of Classroom Expressions, and these expressions have also been utilized in the new exercises so as to make the exercises of more immediately practical use in the classroom.

The new edition contains also fourteen Topical Illustrated Charts with numbered objects. The names of the objects are given in separate lists after the last chart. By thus separating the lists of objects from the charts, the instructor can ask the students to open their books to a chart, and can conduct with the students a great variety of oral Direct-Method exercises, beginning with such simple questions as *¿ Qué es el número uno? ¿ Qué es el número dos?* etc. There was at first some hesitancy on the part of the authors as to whether it would be better to place the respective word lists at the foot of each chart or to place all the lists after the last chart; but it seemed to the authors — and this was also the opinion of teachers who were consulted — that the presence of word lists on the charts would prevent the satisfactory use of the charts in oral Direct-Method work. The students should learn the Spanish names of the objects so that they can give the names without reading them from the lists.

For each Topical Illustrated Chart one page of Direct-Method exercises has been prepared and placed opposite the corresponding chart. These exercises are merely models, and they may be expanded or varied at the pleasure of the teacher. The Classroom Expressions may be used with the first chart, which is a picture of a classroom, or with the objects in the classroom itself.

In general, the authors have aimed to present to English-speaking students the essential facts of Spanish grammar and to illustrate them by means of abundant material for oral and written exercises. The amount of formal grammar given in each Lesson is small, and in the early Lessons there are almost no exceptions to the general rules. At the end of each Lesson the rules of grammar are repeated in Spanish, so that the students may commit them to memory in either Spanish or English, as the teacher prefers.

The words used in the exercises are limited as far as possible to those in common use, and they are given, for the most part, in the connected discourse of descriptive and narrative passages. Each Lesson has a special vocabulary of new words, and at the end of the book there is a general vocabulary which contains all the words that are used in the exercises. The treatment of verbs, which follows the Lessons proper, is unusually complete, and it includes reference lists of irregular verbs and of those that require a preposition before an infinitive.

We wish to acknowledge our indebtedness to many friends for helpful suggestions and advice, and we feel especially indebted to the following: Miss Ellen E. Aldrich, of the editorial department of D. C. Heath & Co.; Mrs. B. E. Bickford, Supervisor of the Teaching of Modern Languages, University High School, Berkeley, California; Dr. Alexander Green, Modern Language Editor, D. C. Heath & Co.; Professor Ralph E. House, of the University of Iowa; Dr. Ramón Jaén, late Assistant Professor of Spanish, University of California; Miss Isabel K. Macdermott, Director of Publications, The Pan-American Union; Professor J. E. Mansion, Modern Language Editor, George G. Harrap & Co., Publishers, London, England; Dr. Federico de Onís, Professor of Spanish, Columbia University; Mrs. Louise Reinhardt, formerly Head of the Department of Modern Languages, Colorado Springs (Colo.) High School; Professor Guillermo Rivera, of Harvard University; Mr. Luis N. Sherwell, formerly Director of the Escuela Normal, Vera Cruz, Mexico, and now teacher of Spanish in the Stuyvesant High School, New York City; and Miss Marie A. Solano, Director of Modern Foreign Languages, Boston, Mass.

E. C. H. AND J. D. M. F.

CONTENTS

v

CONTENTS

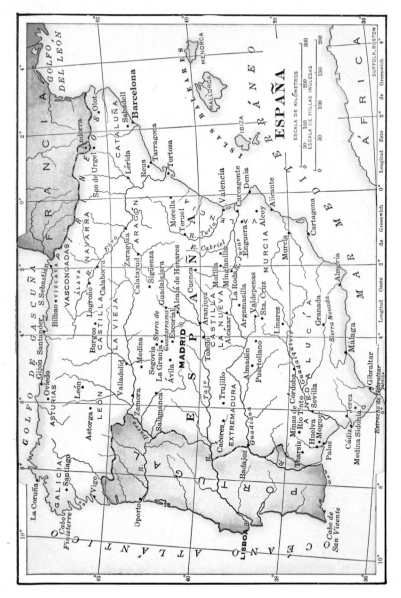

u = *u* of *rule:* **pluma,** *pen.*

The vowels are of medium length or short; they never have the diphthongal sounds heard in the English long *a* (*fate*), long *o* (*no*), etc. There should not be prefixed to **u** the *y* element which it has in such English words as *tube, pure,* etc. In the conjunction **y,** *and,* the sound is that of the simple vowel **i** (*ee*); approximately the same sound is given to final **y,** as in **muy,** *very;* in other positions the **y** has nearly the sound of English *y* in *yet.*

In the western countries of South America, especially in Chile, the final **y** of Castilian is frequently supplanted by **i,** as in **mui** for **muy,** *very,* **i** for **y,** *and,* etc.

4. Vowel Combinations. — When two adjacent vowels in a word combine into a single syllable, they form a diphthong; when three do so, they form a triphthong.

5. Diphthongs. — These are constituted when one of the strong vowels, **a, e, o,** combines with one of the weak vowels, **i, u;** thus,

ai ei oi	au eu ou
ia ie io;	ua ue uo;

or when two weak vowels combine; thus,

iu ui.

If the second element is **i** and occurs at the end of a word, it is written **y,** as in **muy, soy,** etc.

When the syllable containing the diphthong is accented, the stress falls on the strong element, if there be one; otherwise it falls on the second of the two weak vowels.

The various combinations, in an accented syllable, may be illustrated by these words:

baile, *dance;* **hay,** *there is (are)*	**principiamos,** *we begin*
flauta, *flute*	**cuatro,** *four*
reina, *queen;* **rey,** *king*	**bien,** *well*
deuda, *debt*	**fuerte,** *strong*

FIRST SPANISH COURSE

PRONUNCIATION

1. Castilian forms the basis of both the spoken and the written language of cultivated Spaniards and Spanish Americans.

The Alphabet

2. The following list gives the signs comprised in the Spanish or Castilian alphabet with the usual Castilian names for them:

a(*a*), b(*be*), c(*ce*), ch(*che*), d(*de*), e(*e*), f(*efe*), g(*ge*), h(*hache*), i(*i*), j(*jota*), k(*ka*), l(*ele*), ll(*elle*), m(*eme*), n(*ene*), ñ(*eñe*), o(*o*), p(*pe*), q(*cu*), r(*ere*), s(*ese*), t(*te*), u(*u*), v(*ve*, or u *ve*), [w(*doble u*)], x(*equis*), y(*i griega*), z(*zeta* or *zeda*).

Observe that **ch, ll,** and **ñ** figure as distinct signs in the Spanish alphabet. In the dictionary, words and syllables beginning with **ch, ll,** and **ñ** are found after those beginning with **c, l,** and **n** respectively.

3.
VOWELS

a = *a* of *father:* **padre.**

e = (1) *a* of *mate:* **mesa,** *table;* (2) *e* of *met,* before a consonant (except *n* or *s*) in the same syllable, before **rr,** and in the diphthong **ei** (or **ey**) : **papel,** *paper;* **ser,** *to be;* **muerto,** *dead;* **defecto,** *defect;* **perro,** *dog;* **ley,** *law.*

i = *ee* of *meet:* **libro,** *book.*

o = (1) *o* of *note:* **todo,** *all;* (2) *o* of *not* before a consonant in the same syllable, before **rr,** and in the diphthong **oi** (or **oy**) : **sol,** *sun;* **señor,** *sir;* **con,** *with;* **gorra,** *cap;* **soy,** *I am.*

1